T0195792

A SMALL GUIDE TO
Yourself
AND TO YOUR
Dreams

NICOLAS CAHEN

BALBOA.PRESS

A DIVISION OF HAY HOUSE

Balboa Press books may be ordered through booksellers or by contacting:

Balboa Press
A Division of Hay House
1663 Liberty Drive
Bloomington, IN 47403
www.balboapress.com
1 (877) 407-4847

Print information available on the last page.

ISBN: 978-1-9822-4038-7 (sc)
ISBN: 978-1-9822-4037-0 (e)

Balboa Press rev. date: 12/27/2019

CONTENTS

Introduction

Dear reader,

I am happy and excited that you and my book have found each other, and hope it can help you in your life in any way.

My name is Nicolas, 33 years old. Long story short I had a "normal" background for someone born in France in the middle class. Always had food and shelter, went to school and studied till my 20th...

The only difference we could say is that I had the chance the travel a bit, and grew up in some "exotic" places like South Africa and Réunion Island (French colony).

Born in Paris in 1986, at the age of 2 months old my family and I moved to South Africa where we stayed 8 years, probably one of the best memories I have, despite being aparteid (as a young kid in a mix school you don't really realize, not to mention that I had black friends...). Only when you "grown up" do you realise the nonsense of the situation.

After that we went back to France 2 years for some family reasons, then moved to Réunion Island, where I stayed 8 years, it was paradise, a beautiful place to grow up. When

I was 18 years old I decided to move to Paris to study and discover the town I was born in but never lived in.

I stayed there 5 years at first, during those years I was pretty much been a happy person, always done what I wanted and loved with a good degree of integrity, without agreeing with society like a lot of peoples my age I guess.

Somehow this is where my *real* story begins, as I lived my 22 years happily, without really working at school (never really been a good student, didn't like school system), always with good friends and a cool girlfriend.

Sometimes my girlfriend and I travelled between Réunion Island and South Africa, for instance a few days before my final exams we went to South Africa for holiday (house with pool, beach, sun ...), and so I really felt that life was to beautiful. Not preparing for exams, going to holiday instead, being with my girlfriends, basically only doing what I wanted to.

And I thought to myself this cannot continue, it's too good to be true, it cannot last, and not too shortly after that, all fell apart. Obviously didn't get my exams, but also my girlfriend left me. So I had basically lost everything, failed my studies, lost my girlfriend and some friends.

New life

And so I focused on a new life, I really had that mind-set for it (Facebook profile, conversation with friends...), and really left for South Africa, where my family was, and this is where my "new" life begun.

I remember as I was in the car with my mother, enjoying the beauty that Cape town has to offer, I thought to myself "it would be nice to meet friends", for I just arrived, knew nobody and was starting to feel lonely.

Shortly after that I meet my hairdresser that became a dear friend of mine, even if life challenged us, but we are in good terms now.

Let's resume, so far I thought that my old life couldn't continue because it was too beautiful, and it all felt apart. Then I choose to create a new life in Cape Town, which happened. And finally I meet a new friend that I was "asking for"; So many coincidences.

And so this new friend that I that I will call H for privacy, was kind of a spiritual person and often went to trance parties, which are a common thing in South Africa during the summer period. Every summer in Cape Town and others towns you have multiples trance parties per months; it's part of their culture.

This is how I was introduced to trance parties and psychedelics, because the two goes together. I had opportunities to take psychedelics before but never felt like it. But this time, not questions asked, it felt right, it was the right moment.

I've never seen anything alike, it was the first time I ever went to a trance party, I was mesmerized by the environment and the peoples, and couldn't help but to feel that I just entered a magical world. And it is in this environment that I discovered, learned, remembered the truth about myself and the world around. I came to understand thing that were beyond what I could of ever imagined or dreamed of, and this is what I am going to share with you in this book.

The festivals

We arrived at the festival called, "Vortex Easter", in 2010, H and he's friends found a perfect spot, and we started mounting the camp. We then started roaming through the festival, the more we moved deep into it more it become intense, sounds, colors, smells; till we reach the main dance floor which was out of this world.

After talking it all in we keep roaming through the forest, H a friend of he's and I decided to find a discreet spot to stretch and do some yoga before the intake of psychedelics.

The magic started happening on the dance floor, I was around hundred maybe thousands of people, and one of the first things that I noticed is that everybody had s/he own space which was rather pleasant. But with no familiar faces around, I thought about my friend H, and this is where something amazing thing happen, a white light appeared between him and I, in the middle of hundreds of people, I was stunned, I remember going to him and said "I created you here", and he just kept dancing and smiled.

That was probably a turning point in my life, from here on such experiences happened all over the place. When I was negative I would stumble upon something, pump into a negative person, the music would sound chaotic... as when I was positive, I would be offered smokes... I would be offered smokes, drinks, there would be smiles all around, I would find myself surrounded by positive peoples, and the music would sound divine.

I remember to myself this cannot be coincidences, that is when I started to realize that my thoughts created my reality, and the first thing that came to mind was girls; And so I closed my eyes and thoughts about girls, as I opened them back I found myself surrounded by beautiful girls. From that moment on I realized that my thoughts created my reality. Can you imagine what that does to you? It was life changing, to say the least; I had woken up to a certain degree. Plus it was knowledge by acquaintance not by description, it wasn't read or told but experienced, which made it that much more powerful.

At a certain point when watching people there was only light coming out of their eyes, it was amazing, I had the feeling that I had transcended space and time, people at 200m would feel like being right here and some moment seemed eternal.

This was the first festival I ever attended to, not to shortly after a second festival happened called "Acid test v2" (what a coincidence), and there my understanding about myself and the world deepened.

This time I went with H friends, he didn't come with, so during this festival I was more on my own, but didn't mind it as I like being alone and I had plenty of amazing experiences.

For example I learned that my element sign was water through the t-shirt I had (some kind of drops) and intuition, and the element of scorpion which I am is water, (what a coincidence). And I could keep going for hours like that about the understanding of myself and the environment through experiences; It was learning by acquaintance.

I had moment of extreme clarity and presence, and some people would seem so happy to see "some light", I felt like light attracting butterfly, it was strange but pleasant, wanted to help everybody in need.

But the most amazing thing that happen was an **ego death experience.**
It happened on the dance floor, as I was dancing I suddenly realized that I was moving automatically, I was on auto-pilot. I stopped, and became super conscious of myself and the world. I remember looking at the world around me as if it was for the first time.

There was no more thoughts, I was just highly present and aware, it was the most amazing experience of my life. I was so present, conscious, aware that I had transcended my mind and my thoughts.

From that moment on, I "gained" the ability to "watch, observe" my thoughts, like I would look at objects, instead of being identified with them. I'd be more present instead of being sucked in my thought and had more step-back perspective on them. I wouldn't listen or be "controlled" by them, I would be able to observe them. So I understood and realized (at a certain degree) that I was not my ego.

From there on my life had changed, in my day to day life I had control over my mind and understood that it created my reality, it was probably the period I felt the most empowered in my life. All I wanted to do is spread as much knowledge, light and positivity as possible. I was eager to share this knowledge that I had just learned and wanted to share with everyone. It was amazing to say the least.

Then the third official festival arrived. That was also a turning point in my life. It was a festival called "Hysterica", and didn't really feel like going but went anyway.

Well I should have listened to my intuition... It ended up being the worse experience of my life, I kept having ups and downs experiences, sometimes everything was wonderful, full of smiles, I would find friends, and we would be so happy to see each other (it was authentic to a high degree, it was almost soul to soul connection, the ego had dissolved); and in other times I would find my self crying alone in the middle of nowhere in the dark, for no reason, not really knowing who I was. Peoples would laugh at me and I wouldn't find my friends, and if I did I wasn't even able to connect with them, even despite they attempt to help. It was the most unpleasant and confusing experience I ever had. There was that H, all he's friends, and all the amazing people that I had meet at the previous festivals, and I was unable to connect with them, it was a nightmare.

Sadly I ended up being ego lost at quit a high degree. And that lasted for about 5 years (at least)... before I was able to take care of myself again, and choose a healthy life-style, because during those 5 years I had given up. I didn't understood what happened to me, and was frustrated, scared, angry...

I was even afraid of the fact that I created my reality because I had lost control over my thoughts. And one of the result is that I isolated myself from all those I loved for I was afraid to hurt them in any way. Till this day I have to fight constantly to remain aware and not get sucked by thoughts, emotions and fear.

And so I had two festival that putted me on the roof on the world, with a beautiful understanding and the ability to apply it in my day to day life. Helping people energetically and physically, creating the reality of my dream, working on manifesting what I desired, meeting the right people, having the time of my life. It was a revolution of consciousness and mind. But then the third festival got me lost in my mind-thoughts, I got ego-identified.

The desire to understand

Alter all those experiences, now I needed to understand how and why all of this worked the way it did. This is where my journey to understanding and remembering who and what I am, and how the world worked started.

After all those overwhelming events, I wanted to understand how you can create your reality like that and how it worked. I use to only believe in what I see, and had a logical/practical mind. I was on my way to understand how does all of that work.

I've been introduced to the book "The secret" from Rhonda Byrne, which supported my experiences, and that was a best seller, as well as "The power of now" from Eckart tolle. Documentaries like "What the bleep de we know" from William Arntz and many others. So all of that genuine content only confirmed that what I experienced was real and not just the effect of psychedelics.

Then I started hearing about quantum physics that also supported that fact that consciousness, the act of observing changed the behavior of the atomes, in other word, it is physical proof of consciousness over matter.

Everything was falling into place, it was all starting to make sense.

I never believed in god, but now I was believing in the Universe.

I liked the idea that all is one-consciousness, it made sense for me, it resonated with me. If you look at the word Universe. You-niverse, you speak the verse.

You are the one that speak the **verse**. I understood that what we call god is just **all that is**, from the universe, galaxies, planets, any life form, animals, plants, us...

But I wanted to understand more of how it all worked.

And this is what am going to explain in this book.

CHAPTER I

THE IV LAW OF EXISTENCE

This is the content channeled through Daryl Anke by Bashar.

1 - You exist

One/All is the **realization** of existing, of being here and now [Realization I AM].

That is the essence of all that is, **existing, being.**

2 - All is one and one is all

All is one and one is all. [All/one are **unique** and **equal subjective aspect of the one**]

There is only one-consciousness/moment in existence, that consciousness and that infinite and eternal present moment are the same thing; **YOU**-niverse.

All is one infinite and eternal moment/consciousness, experiencing itself subjectively.

3 - What you put out is what you get back

What you put out is what you get back.

The present moment [here and now] is a **mirror**, and it reflect to one, s/he own state of being, energy, frequency of vibration. That state of being is defined by s/he intentions, thoughts, beliefs system, emotions, actions, and focus/attention.

"The inner" (Intentions, thoughts, emotions, beliefs system, actions) is the **reflected** and the "outer" (Physical reality : circumstances, situations, relationships, financial status, health... is the **reflection**.

4 - The only constant is change

The only thing that will never change is change itself, one of the paradox of life.

5 - Personal add-on

All is made of consciousness/energy, vibration at different frequency. And three important factors are **Balance**, **Love and Integrity**.

CHAPTER II

WHO YOU ARE

This is just a reminder, you already know it all, you just have choosen to forget, and now you have decided to remember.

Who are you ?

"You are not a human being having a spiritual experience, you are a spiritual being having a human experience" – Pierre Teilhard de Chardin

I started as an atheist, and through those experiences my perspective and my understanding changed to say the least. I realized at some degree that I was not my ego, so who and what was I ?

I started to realize that I had been giving false beliefs, and that most of society too.

One of those belief is that, who we are is our **ego (body/ mind-thoughts)**, and everything that is attached to it (**name/ age/profession...**).

3

But this isn't true. The ego is a beautiful and complex living organism, it is the avatar, the vessel that allow us to have this experience... but it is not who we are.

So if we are not our ego (body/mind-thoughts), then who and what are we?

To find the answer to this question, it can take many lifetime or a second, either way in my opinion it is THE question that needs answer. To this day I haven't fully realized who I am, my ego still hides in my unconscious, in my habits, in my beliefs, but I know it won't last.

The path to finding the answer to this question as been taken by a lot of philosopher, guru's... and for those that who have found the answer, the answer seems so simple, so obvious.

So this could and should be one of the simplest question there is, and yet most of us struggle to find the answer. This is probably because we never ask the question believing we already know the answer.

Which is understandable for while growing up we've been feed wrong notions about who and what we are, «social conditionning». So we end up believing to be someone/something that we are not.

An other angle to this question is, what remains when we remove the ego (body/mind-thougts) and everything that is attached to it (name, race, job, age...) ?
A natural reaction to this question could be "There is nothing left if I remove all that", and I understand that reaction, I

would done the same, well there might be something left, after all.

«It is only with the heart that one can see rightly; what is essential is invisible to the eye" – Antoine de Saint-Exupery

Close your eyes (if you feel like it), relax, all of your muscles, breath deeply and slowly, and ask this question with genuine intention : Who am I ?

What happen ? Did you find something ? A burst of self-awarerness ?

It's awareness, presence, consciousness, that is who you are.

You see awareness is all that remains when you look above the ego and everything that is attached to it. **You are the realisation of being here and now [I AM]**, that is your essence. You are the witness, the observer behind all mouvement of body and mind, you are pure consciousness, presence.

So there is two main state of being, the state of believing to be your thoughts which I call the "I AM thought", the illusion, impression to be your thoughts. And there is the "I AM sense", which is just the sense of being present, here and now.

Now you can stop for a minute. Try to observe your thoughts as they arise, like you would watch passing cars or clouds, and try not to tap into them.

Through doing that you will start to realise that you are not your thoughts, you will start to realise that there is **the**

one observing the thoughts, You, and the thoughts being observed. **You** are real, but the thoughs are not.

This realisation can take time but don't worry, I believe it's part of the game of life, we deliberately putted ourselves in a state of amnesia so we could remember who we are through experiences.

There is a few existing practices that can help you remember who you are, we are going to discuss them in the coming parts.

- Here's an analogy than might be helpful to break free from the mental.

There is a screen that represent consciousness (you), and there is a movie that represent reality (world/body/mind-thoughts...), the screen is real and always here and now, while the movie is not real, and has a beginning and an end. You see your body (if you believe in reincarcaion), thoughts and emotions comes and goes while you are ever present.

We could even push the analogy further and say that the higher the degree of consciousness, the bigger and clearer the screen. **In a way the level of consciousness defines the quality of perception.**

- Here's a quote that put that in perspective.

"If you have a golf-ball-sized consciousness, when you read a book, you'll have a golf-ball-sized understanding; when you look out a golf-ball-sized awareness, and when you wake up in the morning, a golf-ball-sized wakefulness.

But if you could expand that consciousness, then you read that book more understanding; you look out, more awareness, and when you wake up, more wakefulness." - David Lynch

«The quieter the mind, the greater the level of consciousness.» -Cahen Nicolas

So to conclude, you are not your ego (body, feelings, mind-thoughts), you are the presence, awareness, consciousness that witness it, observe it, that animate it.

You are the creator and the ego and the word is the creation.

How to be who you are?

"The ego paradox: It exist but it's not real, like a mirage, the phenomena of the mirage exist, but what the mirage shows isn't real, it's an illusion".

A flower doesn't have to do anything to be a flower, it just is.

The same way you don't have to do anything to be who you are, you are already it. Beingness is your nature, and to be is effortless (like breathing, seeing, hearing, feeling but even easier). **We are already what we seek to be.**

"Self-realization is effortless. What you are trying to find is what you already are." -Ramesh S Balsekar

The real question should be, "how to remove the illusion to not be you".

Who you are is right here and now, only the movement of the mind and the belief that you are it, prevent you from seeing/realizing YOU. So the only thing that can give you the illusion of not being you, is the belief to be something you are not, in our case the ego (body/mind/thoughts).

You don't have to think, you don't have to act, you just are who you are by being. Thinking is what actually what prevent you from realizing who you are.

Here are techniques that can help you realize who you are (this part come from the ego chapter, for breaking identification with the ego and realizing who you are the same thing).

First technique

One of the most well known and advised method, which is a form of meditation, is to pratice to acknowled and **observe** your thoughts as they arise, without identifying with them, keeping a stepback perspective.

That means without judging, attacking... them, no matter how uncomfortable. Just let them happen/flow and witness them without giving them your attention, just be aware of them (like hearing instead of listening, seeing instead of watching...), and don't react to them.

This is done because you cannot get ride or destroy thoughts, all you can do is *watch them* and realise that they are not who you are. Fighting it only reinforces the illusion that it is real. Through doing that eventually you will be more conscious of your thoughts, slowly realise that you are not then and you will gain the ability to choose them consciously.

Be especially aware of the "I" thought, for it is the source of all thoughts, if you identify with it, you identify with all thoughts, this is what I call the "I am thought". So try to spot the «I» thought as it arise, *and observe it, watch it instead of identifying with it.*

But never condemn your "I" thoughts or any thoughts for that matter, just remain present, aware and allow them to flow, this should be one of the most effortless practice (if you put any effort into it, mentally or any other way, you got it wrong, **you are already who you are, you have nothing to do but to be,** it's just about realising what you are not), just relax, sit back and watch your thoughts, the same way you would watch a movie, or clouds in the sky, and slowly realise that they are not you.

Through doing that you stop «feeding» your thoughts with attention (for attention is energy), and eventually you will start to break identification with your thoughts, you will begin to realize that there is the **one observing the thoughts (You)**, and the **thoughts being observed**. You will developpe something I call the «I AM sense», which is just the sense of being present, here and now.

So you will go from the «I am thoughts» state, which is the sense of being your thoughts, "I am this I am that", to the «I AM sense» which is once gain just the sense of being present, here and now. Switching between «I AM thoughts» to «I AM sense», that is liberation.

So like I said eventually your awareness will dissolve your identification, you will become more aware, present, conscious and your attention will be more directed to the present moment, rather than to your thoughts, you will become more for self-aware, self-conscious but also more conscious of your environment.

The more you practice the more the degree of realization will increase, awareness/consciousness is like a muscle, the more you practice the more is develops. Consistency is key here.

Second technique

This methode is not as organic as the first one and should be used with moderation.

The idea is to practice speaking and thinking without first person pronouns (I, me). Going strait to the point, you will realize how you over-strain first person pronouns and you will realize that they are not as required as you assume.

For examples:

"Going to buy some food" instead of "I am going to buy some food"

"You did very well" instead of "I thought you did very well"

"It feel so good to be her" instead of "I am so happy to be her"

Through doing that we are less stimulating the ego, and we are actually more into what we are actually talking about and the present moment.

[There will be more content about how to break identification with the Ego in the "Ego" chapter]."

Conclusion

Remember you are already who you are just, always been, will always be, just remain present, silent, and as you are silent, and as thoughts arise (because they probably will), just observe them, watch them, and remain present.

Don't judge yourself, don't judge your thoughts, don't judge others and don't judge the world, it will allow you see things for what they really are, and not what you think they are.

Characteristics of our true nature

"If you want to unlock the secret of the universe, you need to think in terms of energy, vibration and frequency". - Nikola Tesla

We are vibration

At the deepest level of creation, all is vibrations at different frequencies, The Universe, us and our body-mind/thoughts included. This is has been proven by modern physics (Quantum mechanics).

The world is an ocean of vibrating consciousness, made of infinite different frequencies... From matter to light and probably beyond.

We are space-less and timeless

Space and time don't exist, they are only mental construct.

Past is a memory of something that happened **now** but that is over.

Future is a projection of your mind about something that might happen **now** but hasn't yet.

So in both cases they are mental construct, they are not real, **now**, the present moment is. So our deepest nature is space-less, timeless (consciousness operate outside the space/time field which is a mental construct). In other words we are infinite and eternal beings. Our ego's will die, but who we truly are will live forever, in this infinite and eternal present moment.

We are formless and nameless

As it as been said previously said, our true nature is not the body and the mind, that means that we have no form, no name, no age...

Names remains label made by the mind, the closest you can come to put a name on who you are is "I AM that I AM", which is basically stating that I am the realization I am.

We are one

Everything is one consciousness/moment [Realization I AM] having a subjectively experience of itself, through the infinite possibility of dreams and imagination. Each subjective aspect is just a different perspective, point of view of source, one-consciousness, YOU.

We are all mirrors of each other

Every subjective aspect work as a mirror for each other, we all reflect each other. Life is a hall of mirror, all there is is **YOU**.
We are all the same consciousness into different bodies and we all are reflection on each other.

The world is inside YOU [You-niverse]

Don't forget that all of this is a **self created imagined world, it's all a dream**. You are not in the world, the world in inside **You**. World/body/mind/thoughts/emotions exist within the one-consciousness [I AM/YOU], and arise from the projection of the one-consciousness dream/imagination. **So you don't exist within physical reality but physical reality exist within you.**

Believing being the body/mind/thoughts is dreaming within a dream.

Conclusion

One is not and cannot be s/he (body if one believe in reincarnation) thoughts/emotions because they come and go and one is always here and now, present. One is just pure consciousness.

CHAPTER III

EGO

What is the ego ?

As said in the previous chapter the ego is the body/mind-thoughts structure, which is a perfect piece of living organic and vibratory technology (probably the most advanced piece of technology on earth).

It is what allows consciousness, (you/I/all) to experience this reality as *humans*, it is what allow us to have a subjective/personal experience (for all is one consciousness), it is our avatar, our vessel.

Having a human experience is the result of consciousness (you/I/all) merging with the ego (body/mind-thoughts). Once a soul as merged with the ego, it gain access to all the features it has to offer, and the experiences that comes with it. Hearing, touching, seeing, tasting, smelling through the five senses of the body, focusing, thinking... through the mind, walking, creating, talking... through the members and organes of the body. Those experiences coudn't be achieved without the ego (for by nature we, consciousness, can only **be**.)

From the leve of human experience, the same thing as been done, we created tools that allows us to have certain experiences that we coudn't have without them.

Cars allow us to move fasted, planes allow us to fly and travel further and quicker, computers and phones allows us to communicate with each without being bound by space and time.

An other interesting aspect is that the ego we have is not chosen at random. Like it as been said we are all one consciousness experiencing itself subjectively, and each subjective aspect which is you, I and all, are unique and complete each others, alike pieces of a puzzle, when putted together they are complete.

Well our ego's reflect that, they are unique as well, they all have unique features, finger print, eyes, DNA... And so as souls we don't just pick a random ego, we create the ego that is best suited for us, **a unique ego for a unique soul, for unique experiences.**

But not only do we choose our ego's, but also all the major events that happen through out our lives, the set and setting, environment (family, partners, friends, country...) in which we experience, grow and evolve... in order to get the experience we deemed the best for our re-memberence.

So after merging with the ego you benefit from all the features it provides, (walking, talking, hearing, smelling, touching, seeing, thinking...) but you are not it, the ego serves you as a vehicle, it allows you to go from a to b (and more). And like you are not your car, you are not your ego.

A SMALL GUIDE TO YOURSELF AND TO YOUR DREAMS

"The ego is not the owner of consciousness, it is the object" -Sartre

The ego setup

The ego is comparable to a computer, it as a hardware aspect (body) and a software aspect (mind), and there is the user (you).

Body - >	System unit
Brain ->	CPU
Eyes ->	Graphic card
Ears ->	Sound card
Mind ->	Operating system (OS)

The ego works the same way than your computer, it needs to be configured/setup, and personalized to your own preferences.

To setup your computer you install an OS (Windows), drivers, default software (usually it's done for you) and then you personalize it with software's, data (files, music, movies, pictures, wallpaper, favorites...).

Well it work a bit the same with your ego, it as being setup since it's birth (conditioning), it as been taught to speak, write, read, count, and then you personalize it with skill, interest, beliefs, values, ideas, thoughts that fits your preferences and personality.

And depending of the choices you made in the selection of your skill, interest ... your life is oriented in a specific direction.

The problem is that some of those beliefs, values, ideas... are setup by a third party that doesn't always have your best interest at heart, and that's conditioning.

The conditioning of the ego

The ego is often seen as the issue, but it's not, it's how we use it, like everything else, **it's not what but how you use it**.

In today's society our ego are conditioned since birth by the *elite community* (governments, corporations, lobby's, banks) in an attempt to make us more controllable, manageable, obedient, docile, we are made smart enough to do the work and shortsighted enough to not question the system.

The reason for that is because they are power, greed ego driven. So obviously not only do they diffuse wrong ideas, values ... but they run them too. It is basically the same, ego-based "ME" before "WE" mind-set, except they are running some "super-ego settings" and they are diffusing some "victim-ego settings" manner of speaking.

So they function on wrong values (Low politic integrity, corporate greed) and they diffuse the same values (ego-based values, capitalist values...).

The way through which they diffuse those wrong and limiting ideas, values, principals... that are based on ignorance and fear is through media (media lobby are owned by government or are strongly influenced by it), religion, school (which is more of a ship farm than an schools), parenting (themselves sadly have been conditioned)...

We have been raised as cattle and we've been lied to, the truth kept away.

The way this manifest is in creating a story which is the mainstream narrative, and the story goes something like that:

- You are your body/mind-thoughts, and you will die (or go to heaven or hell if one is religious).
- You are your name, your age, your job, your race...
- Reality/life just happen to you, and there is nothing you can about it.
- We don't know where we came from, why we are here.

Peoples listen because they haven't found anything better, and that everybody seems to follow the same mainstream narrative. And so if you apply this in your life your belief system would look something like that: "**I am my body, mind, thoughts,**" and everything that comes with it "**I am that religion, I am from that social class, I am from that race, I am that name...**"

Those ideas makes you compliant to authority and obedient because if you listen to them you are the result of hazard and have no real purpose. And so you kind a become they puppet.

When science actually show us that there is more than meet the eye, there is starting to have proof that consciousness survive the ego's death, and so could be an after world, and it is my belief that we are soul incarnating on earth to be ourselves, learn, have experiences... and that we all have something unique and magic to add to the world.

But because the MN (mainstream) is the loudest, and that everybody listen to it, probably you included... I mean to be honest we've all been conditioned, now it is up to us to either wake up and take the driver site or go with the MN all our lives... which would be so sad.

If you listen to the MN story, it makes you disconnected from the truth, from yourself, and from your soul purpose, your soul plan, you become a sheep.

So when you listen to that narrative and follow the default society model, you have a life that looks something like that: Go to School, study, find a job (if you are lucky one that you don't hate it), buy a house/car, make a family, pay your bills, taxes, credits...
This is the **mental aspect** of conditioning, but there is also the **physical aspect**, nutrition. This is more the field of corporation but it's largely supported by government (they work hand in hand, the purpose always having more power, more money and making people unconscious).

Diseases

For instance the institution of diabetes in America is sponsored by fast food chains (when the first cause of diabetes is unhealthy food, meat...)

Institution that are supposed to protect the people have been corrupted by the *elite community* (corporations, lobby's, banks, governments).

For example the heath industry and the educative system in most countries have been infiltrated and corrupted. Not to mention that schools and hospitals are structures that are run-ed and controlled by government which are highly influenced by corporations.

What is though in school is not what best benefit the individual or collective. The educative program designed follows and agenda of the elite, and is true at any degree of education, from primary to doctoral degree, for example doctors are not though to cure diseases but to cure symptoms. Cancer is an billion dollars industry, like many other diseases, no wonder that doctors are not though to cure it. We could easily cure most diseases today.

People that self medicate through vegan based diet, CBD... succeed in recovering from cancers when they were diagnosed in final stage... Even patient without cancer are diagnostic with it, as chemotherapy is a massive source of profit...

Diet

There is also notions such as meat, eggs and dairy are required to be healthy, ideas that are spread by corporation through government (school, doctors...). When it as actually been proven by science that they are one of the first cause of cancer, stroke, diabetes... Once again, profit before human lives.

"The high level of meat and saturated fat consumption in the USA and other high-income countries exceeds nutritional needs and contributes to high rates of chronic diseases such as cardiovascular disease, diabetes mellitus and some cancers." — Polly Walker

The only reason those false statement persists is simply because those are huge lobby worth billions who work hand in hand with governments and that are overpowered. The reason for that is because we **buy** they product, we are the source of their power.

Meat, dairy, pharmaceutic, media are all industries that have been infiltrated/infected by ego greed mind-set. Not to mention the negative impact of the production of meat and dairy on the environment...

But that's not all, now there is alcohol, cigarettes, GMOs... who are also lobby working with the government, and they product is very detrimental to your health and to the environment.

So by combining the conditioning of the mental aspect and the physical aspect, that gives you a simple-minded, obedient individual that don't ask question and don't question authority.

The conditioning of the ego should be based on **integrity and on good intention** as to make the soul/consciousness thrive. Sadly in our society conditioning is mostly based on fear and ignorance that makes the soul/consciousness diminish and lessen...

Today most human beings have been lobotomized, and are unconscious has to who they really are, and what they real history is, they have been deprived from true knowledge, and given a fake identities and story's.

So we've established that our egos have being conditioned since birth in a way that doesn't always serve/benefits us as an individual and as a collective, for some of those ideas, values... are self chosen, and some are imposed by a third party that doesn't always have our best interest at heart. But the good news is that we don't have to accept those ideas ... we can choose/create our own.

Identification with the ego (symptom of conditioning)

Identification with the ego is the **belief to be your body, mind and thoughts.**

This phenomena is usually the result of growing up in a certain environment (school, parenting, media, friends...), and by being exposed to certain things like cultures, religions, mainstream narrative... all together they can create some kind of marinade that if we stay to long in to we really take in the flavor, manner of speaking.

By being constantly exposed throughout our live to that environment and to the cultures, regions and mainstream narrative, that promote individualism, capitalism and wrong ideas, we develop a false idea of who and what we are, a false mental sense of identity around all the ideas, beliefs, labels that comes from the combination of all those factors

23

(environment, culture, religion, school, media, parenting, social life...).

Like said in the "The conditioning of the ego" it create a story that we usually end up believing, and it does something like that: "My name is John, I am Christian, I am American, I need to buy to feel content, I am allowed this but not that, I must behave like this, I am Caucasian, I am republican, I am middle class, I am electrician..."

After repeating that story over and over in our heads, the "I thought sense" develops, **it is the impression to be the thought «I»**, and quit literally you then develop a sense of being your thoughts. So instead of seeing them as external extension of you believe to be them. It's like if you would believe to be your phone or your car. This is the result of overfeeding your thoughts with your energy, through giving it too much attention and listing to it (attention is energy).

If one atteint a high level of identification then every intention, decision, action will directly be followed by the thought "I". So instead of doing something, and remaining mostly focused in the present, you think "I am going to do this, that... this is wrong this is right..." and remaining mostly in your thoughts.

The consequences of identification with the ego

Identification with the ego is the source of all misery and suffering of humanity.

A SMALL GUIDE TO YOURSELF AND TO YOUR DREAMS

If you operate from a state where we are identified with your thoughts, you lose the step back perspective on your thoughts where you see them objectively as external object, and you are **head into them and can't differentiate you from them**.

In such a state you lose touch with reality and with your ability to shape it the way you prefer, for you get run by your ego, your half-conscious, conditioning and compulsive thinking. It's kind like being in a coma, your consciousness is sucked into your thoughts, and instead of perceiving reality from here and now, you perceive it from your "thoughts zone" (judgment label, time...).

Another consequence when you are identified with your thoughts, is that they (especially judgments and labels) act as filters on reality, **what IS** (which include yourself, others and the world), and usually "provide" a distorted version of it. It's like superposing a fake version of reality upon reality.

In truth nothing is good, bad, ugly, pretty... everything just IS.

Good, bad, ugly, pretty... are only notion that exist in contrast to/through the mind, but if you remove the mind then everything just IS.

When you judge or label something or someone, it doesn't make **what IS** into **what you think IS.** It just make you perceive **your** version of reality. In truth **what IS** (reality) hasn't changed, so end of the day you just misperceive reality.

For example, a piece of art judged by two parties, one deems it pretty the other ugly but neither are right, for the piece of art **just is** what it is.

Not to mention that judgments and labels are usually based on limitation, separation, fear, ignorance... So an advice, don't judge yourself, others and the world; It will help you perceive things as they really are.

When people are identified with their thoughts, it create some kind of ego individualism ego mode where they forget that they are part of the one-consciousness and believe to be separated from the rest. And so at the result everybody fights for survival.

So you can now understand why people are so depressed, and why the world is in such a state. One doesn't think as a whole anymore but as an isolated and separated individual, "WE" becomes "ME", this is a great source of suffering.

We can see that this state is very present in today's world, especially in the western culture, peopled are very egocentric, it's all about me, they don't like sharing, there is little compassion... this is true for people as well as corporation and government.

Here's are few examples that we can witness with people and in organization, corporation...

  – Food surplus in restaurant and supermarket is thrown away (instead of being given to people in need).
  – People sleep in the street without bed when you have bed without people in shops. This can seem silly, but

it's a blatant example that in today's society money as more value than human lives.
- People rarely share or help people in need, in the street, or in general.

But because we have been so well misconditioned, and evolve in a world where those things are "normal" we exhibit and accept such wrong behavior as if it were normal.

This explain why the world is in such a state (famine, war, poverty, depression, anxiety...). People are unconscious about they ability to shape the reality they desire (coming in next chapter : Reality), and they identify with they thoughts and perceive reality through the filters of judgment.

How to break free from identification with the ego

The paradox of the ego : It's an illusion but it exist, like the mirage, the phenom of the mirage exist, but what the mirage shows don't.

To break identification with the ego is to **stop believing that you are your thoughts and body**. Doing that can be referred to as **enlightenment.** The realization that the ego is not who we are, that it's not real.

There is different methods, tools, techniques, practices that can help you break free from identification with your ego.

First method

One of the most well known and advised method, which is a form of meditation, is pratice to acknowled and **observe** your thoughts as they arise, without identifying with them.

That means without judging, attacking... them, no matter how uncomfortable. Just let them happen/flow and witness them without giving them your attention, just be aware of them (like hearing instead of listening, seeing instead of watching...), and don't react to them.

This is done because you cannot get rid or destroy thoughts, all you can do is *watch them* and realize that they are not who you are, fighting it only reinforces the illusion that it is real. Through doing that eventually you will be more conscious of your thoughts, and will gain the ability to choose them consciously.

Be especially aware of the "I" thought, for it is the source of all thoughts, if you identify with it you identify with all thoughts, this is what I call the "I am thought". So try to spot the «I thought» as it arise, *and observe it, watch it instead of identifying with it.*

But never condemn it or any thoughts for that matter, just remain present, aware and allow them to flow, this should be one of the most effortless practice (if you put any effort into it, mentally or any other way, you got it wrong, **you are already who you are, you have nothing to do but to be,** it's just about realizing what you are not), just relax, sit back and watch your thoughts, the same way you would watch a movie, or clouds in the sky, and slowly realize that they are not you.

Through doing that you stop «feeding» your thoughts with attention (for attention is energy), and eventually you will start to break identification with your thoughts, you will begin to realize that there is the **one observing the thoughts (You)**, and the **thoughts being observed**. You will develop the «I AM sense», which is just the sense of being present, here and now.

So you will go from the «I am thoughts» state which is the sense of being your thoughts, "I am this I am that", to the «I AM sense», once again just the sense of being here and now. Switching from «I AM thoughts» to «I AM sense», that is liberation.

So like I said eventually your awareness will dissolve your identification, you will become more aware, present, conscious and your attention will be more directed to the present moment, rather than to your thoughts, you will become more for self-aware, self-conscious, but also more concsious of your environment.

The more you practice the more the degree of realization will increase, awareness/consciousness is like a muscle, the more you practice the more is develops, consistency is key here.

Second method

This method is not as organic as the first one and should be used with moderation.

It's about practicing speaking and thinking without first person pronouns (I, me). It's about going straight to the point of what you want to say, you will realize that you over-strain first person pronouns and that they are not as required as you assume. Not to mention that it is an exercise of consciousness, it pushes you to be more aware of your thoughts.

For example:

"Going to buy some food" instead of "I am going to buy some food"

"You did very well" instead of "I thought you did very well"*

"This is wonderful" instead of "I think this is wonderful"

Food for thoughts?

This might sound a bit silly but it might help.

The ego which is body/mind/thoughts is temporary, like everything that exist in this universe, it has a beginning and an end, except for consciousness. And so thoughts/emotions/body (if you believe in reincarnation) comes and goes, but you are always here and now, so here's the question.

How can you be something can come and goes (thoughts/emotions/body), if you are always here and now?

Visualization

The following analogy can be used as a visualization exercise.

Imagine yourself as being a huge rock, present, here and now, and your thoughts and emotions (past, future...) as a hurricane, no matter how strong the wind blows, you do not move, you remain present. It's about remaining anchored in the present moment even (especially) when thoughts and emotions arise.

Practices

There is different practices that can help you be more aware of your thoughts, and increase your degree of consciousness, such as meditation, breath work, yoga...

Any activities that take you attention into the present moment.

I invite you to make some research about the practices that feels right for you, it can be anything, sport, music, art, music, writing... but meditation and yoga are good starting point.

Diet & lifestyle

"You are what you eat", we all heard that saying.

Diet and exercise are great tools than can help you improve your state of being, and which can be a game changer, for food and exercise influence greatly the body and the mind, healthy life-style is a game changer.

- When you exercise, eat healthy, organic plant-based diet (preferably), have an intake of sunlight every day for about 15m (vitamins D), it stimulate noble things like learning, reading, more exercising, organizing, cleaning... and your mind is more calm and grounded.

– As if you don't exercise and eat, junk food, meat, have not sunlight... it stimulate lower instincts such as procrastination, watching TV, no willingness for exercise, smoking, drinking ...

When on a healthy life-style you will quickly realize the difference, your mind will be clearer, you will feel good, full of energy and probably be willing to start new sports, business, take on projects, opportunities...

Alkaline vs Acid

An interesting fact, that has been hidden from the public (Like Nikola Tesla for free energy or Stanley Allen Meyer for the water engine) is the discovery of Dr. Otto Warnurg

"Every single person who has cancer has a pH that is too acidic," -Dr. Otto Warnurg

"won the Nobel Prize in 1931 for proving that cancer can't survive in an alkaline oxygen rich environment but thrives in an acidic, low oxygen environment."

So that means that if you maintain an **Alkaline based diet you will never have cancer, or any disease** for that matter, what an amazing fact, specially knowing that there is a billion dollars industry based on cancer that is running)...

Examples of food that are Acid : Meat, fish, alcohol, dairy, soda....

Examples of food that are Alkaline : Lemons, mangoes, garlic, vegetables....

Doshas

I would also to introduce to you the idea of **Doshas**, which is one of three substances that are present in a person's body according to Ayurveda (Indian medecine system).

Here are the three Doshas :

VATA : Space and Air
PITTA : Fire and Water
KAPHA : Water and Earth

You take a MCQ test, it's easily to find on internet. After taking the MCQ you will know your Doshas. Depending on the result you will have a certain diet that is proposed, which is designed to balance you out.

So for example I am mainly VATTA and a bit PITTA, which mean that I am mostly space, air and a bit water and fire, which make me unstable (I used to be called the boy with the head in the moon when I was a kid), and so I am recommended to eat warm, comforting, heavy food to ground me. It is better for me to eat food that grows in the earth, like potatoes, carrots... On the other side KAPHA must eat light food like vegetables... because they are very grounded, I think you get the idea.

The pineal gland

Finally I wanted to introduce to you the idea of **pineal gland** if you are not already familiar with it. The Pineal gland is also called the third eye, the site of the soul, it is what the eye of Horus represent.

With the life-style of the mainstream your pineal gland get calcify (litteraly, is deactivated it, thought fluorine which is present in water, tooth paste. But there is also other product that are detrimental to your pineal gland like industrial food, alcohol, tobacco...). By having a healthy life-style you decalcify and activate your Pineal gland.

Here are things that you can do to decalcify your pineal gland:

Sun gazing: Watching the first 5 minute as the sun rise and set for it it not harmful for the eyes at that level. You should start with 10 second every sunrise and every sunset and increase 10 second everyday.
Healthy diet: Having a organic plant-based diet help tremendously your Pineal gland to decalcify and activate.
Filter your water: Water is a great source of fluorine, even in bottle. Get a filter if you can, they are not too expensive.
Toothpaste: Use alternative, fluoride-free toothpaste.
Melatonin: A cure of 1 month of Melatonin before sleeping can help in activating the Pineal gland.
Raw cacao: **Raw**, **organic** chocolate in its purest form can help detoxify the **Pineal gland** because of **cacao's** high antioxidant content. **Cacao** will also help stimulate the third eye.

But I invite you to make your own research as to find what best suit you.

End of your day you diet & life style plays an important part in the well being of body, mind and soul. I believe having a healthy routine each morning is key. For example here's my routine:

- Wake up around 7h
- 1 big glass of water first thing
- 1 big glass on water and lemon
- Meditation for about 20m (Increase slowly)
- Break first, smoothie, muesli, nuts, supplement (spirulina, nootropics which are cognitive enhancement, better focus, memory, clarity, any supplement that feel right for you if any.
- Will sun bath for 20m for energy and vitamin D
- Exercise for 1h and shower.
- Get all the paper work of the day sorted, be up to date with projects, peoples ...

If you do that you will be amazed by the feel good state and the productivity.

Give it a try, you have nothing to lose.

Psychedelics

I am not suggesting the intake of those substances, I am just pointing out the fact that they have been recognize as having some consciousness-expanding effect.

MDMA, LSD and magic mushroom have been approved by the FDA as a potential treatment for PTSD and other disorder.

Psychedelics has been used throughout the ages by most ancient civilization (Maya, Inca, Egyptian...) with always a connection to the divine.

In my opinion psychedelics are tools of evolution/remembrance putted on earth by ourselves as reminders of who and what we are, and why you are here, to raise our level of consciousness.

If it's the right substance, with the right dosage in the right set and setting there is a high probability that it leave long term positive changes. It as been proven that psychedelics stimulate something called neuroplasticity, which facilitate the create for new pathways in your brain.

Here are a few example of psychedelics: LSD, Mushroom, Ayahuasca, Peyote...

Observe your breathing

Breath is always occurring, from birth to death, with or without thoughts. It could be seen as a conductive thread to the present moment.

Bring your attention to your breathing, let your body do the work, all you have to do is relax and observe your breathing, it will always bring you back to the present moment.

Sounds

We are vibratory beings, and music, sounds can have an important influence on us.

There are different frequencies that are known to help to harmonize the body.

Earth frequency 136.1hz : Tuned the Earth frequency of **136.1Hz**, the Ohm Tuner (also referred to as mid-ohm) helps to release strain and stress in the heart. Use it when your energy is low, you feel a lack of connectedness, unable to focus and concentrate or feel need to ground Tuned the Earth frequency of **136.1Hz**, the Ohm Tuner (also referred to as mid-ohm) helps to release strain and stress in the heart. Use it when your energy is low, you feel a lack of connectedness, unable to focus and concentrate or feel need to ground.

Pythagoras scale 432hz : Musical therapy helps ease anxiety, bring down heart rate and blood pressure, and generally has a soothing effect.

Shuman resonance 7.83Hz : It has been proven by scientific experiments that tuning into 7.83Hz, the planet's own magnetic frequency people experience benefits like enhanced learning/**memory**, body rejuvenation, **balance**, improved **stress** tolerance, **anti**-jetlag, **anti**-mind control, and grounding.

Brain waves :

Gamma / 38 – 42 Hz	Brain waves are the fastest and are associated with higher levels of consciousness.
Beta / 12 – 38 Hz	Waves are the most common pattern in the normal waking state. They occur when one is alert and focused on problem solving.
Alpha / 8 – 12 Hz	Waves occur during quiet, thoughtful times. Alpha waves indicate that the brain is in a resting state.
Theta / 3 – 8 Hz	Waves also occur in sleep and during relaxation. They are indicative of an inner focus, and dreams and vivid imagery occur in this state.
Delta / 0,5 – 3 Hz	Brain waves are the slowest brain waves. They are generated in deep meditation and dreamless sleep. Healing and regeneration occur when the brain is in this state.

Solfeggio frequencies

Solfeggio frequencies make up the ancient (main) 7-tone scale thought to have been used in sacred music, including the beautiful and well known Gregorian Chants. The chants and their special tones were believed to impart spiritual blessings when sung in harmony. Each Solfeggio tone is comprised of a frequency required to balance your energy and keep your body, mind and spirit in perfect harmony.

Here are the seven main solfeggio frequencies:

UT – 396 Hz – Transforming grief into joy and guilt, fear into forgiveness.

RE – 417 Hz – Clears negativity and removes subconscious blockages. Helps in undoing situations and facilitating change,

MI – 528 Hz – Stimulates love, restores equilibrium, repairs DNA. Evidence suggests that this frequency has the potential to positively affect cellular water clusters to assist in removing impurities to prevent sickness and disease.

FA – 639 Hz – Re-connect, balance and strengthens relationships, family, and community unity.

SOL – 741 Hz – Physically cleanses the body from all types of toxins as well as solving problems, expressions/solutions

LA – 852 Hz – Awakens intuition and helps you return to spiritual balance.

SI – 963 Hz - It awakens any system to its original, perfect state. When it is applied to a cell, it enables a kind of "cellular enlightenment" and transformation of the cell to a higher level. Helps us return to Oneness -to our very source.

When we talk about the **benefits** of the ancient Solfeggio frequencies, we often talk in terms of their spiritual, psychological, and other non-material effects.

Chakras & crystals

Chakras represent each of seven centers of spiritual power in the human body.

Root chakra	Red	Basic trust
Sacral chakra	Orange	Sexuality, creativity
Solar plexus chakra	Yellow	Wisom, power
Heart chakra	Green	Love, healing
Throat chakra	Blue	Communication
Third eye chakra	Indigo	Awareness
Crown chakra	Purple	Spirituality

When not all open is create disease and disharmony at all level of your being, physically, mentally, emotionally, spirituality.

Crystals have the ability to help unlock those Chakras, each Chakras has a set a crytals that are beneficial for them. For example the Ametyst works well with the Crown chakra. Usually the color of the crystals and the chakras match.

I invite you to make your own research on Chakras if you are interested by it.

Numerology & Astrology

Believe in it or not, but after reading this book, I believe you will be more open minded toward those type of science.

A SMALL GUIDE TO YOURSELF AND TO YOUR DREAMS

Numerology: **Numerology** is any belief in the divine or mystical relationship between a number and one or more coinciding events. It is also the study of the numerical value of the letters in words, names, and ideas. It is often associated with the paranormal, alongside astrology and similar divinatory arts

Here is the formula to calculate your number.

- Write your birth date in numbers for example 06/11/1986 which is my birthday.
- Add the numbers in the year together: 1+9+8+6.
- Add the month and day of birth to the year number: 6+11+24 = 41.
- Add the end result together to obtain a one-digit number: 4+1=5.

So the number is 5 which is adventurous, seeker, and teacher of esoteric wisdom, sensual, addictive traits. Usually numbers and for zodiac signs correlate, and share some specifics (and it does in this case).

I invite you to make your own research regarding the meaning of the 9 numbers.

Usually numbers and for zodiac signs correlate, and share same specifics.

This can help you know yourself better and work and the aspect that needs to.

Self-conditioning

We've been conditioned since birth by the elite community, with ideas, values, principles that doesn't serve us as individual or as collective, but that means that **we can re-conditioned** ourselves, here is different tips that can help you in doing that :

Dream-board: It allows us to visualize what you desire, and so it make it more, tangible, approachable to you.

Positive affirmation: "I am worthy, I will succeed, I can do it..." by doing that daily it help you maintain positive and confidant state of being and actually create new neuro-pathways.

Gratitude: In terms of frequencies, gratitude is the opposite of wanting, wanting is a frequency of lack, and it only brings you more wanting/lack. As gratitude is a frequency of abundance and bring you more things to be grateful for.

Focusing only on things that passionate and excite you: Attention is water, what you give it to will grow, so chose carefully what you give you attention (attention is energy) to. And you can apply this with everything, people, activities, ideas...

What not to do

Don't attack, judge... your thoughts because by doing so you only reinforces the illusion that they exist, so just step-back and observe from a far like said previously and keep breaking through identification.

Conclusion

I've let my mind and it's conditioning prevent me from seeing and enjoying this magical world for to long, please don't let that happen to you to.

All of those methods, practices, techniques ... are tools to help you breakthrough your identification with the mind and it's thoughts. And through that remembering/realizing who you are, and what you are here to do.

CHAPTER IV

REALITY

What is reality?

At the deepest level, reality is **what IS.**

YOU, the present moment is the same thing, **what IS.**

But then from YOU and your imagination (**I-magi-nation**)... emerged the **YOU**-niverse. The Universe is your creation.

There is YOU the dreamer (I AM consciousness) who's nature is just to "exist, here and now", and there is the dream (the world around You). Which also just "exist", here and now" but is just a dream. Everything exist here and now, even in nowhere there is now-here.

To make an analogy the dreamer (you) is the screen (real), and the dream is the movie (not real), so the dreamer (you) is real, and the dream (the ego, world, universe) is not.

This idea is starting to be agreed on by quantum physics as well as a few known people, Elon musk... all agree to say that the world around use is **holographic.**

Elon Musk said in one of he's interview that there is a high probability that we are in a simulated video game, which is another way of saying that we are in a dream, "holographic reality".

So this might be a big pill to swallow but to sum things up, we are all one consciousness dreaming what we call "reality", and this dream allows subjectivity, self-experience.

So the universe is a self dreamed, created holographic environment for self experience.

Another logic but interesting fact is that **you don't exist within the world, the world exist within you**, it is your dream after all.

Game analogy

- World -> Map
- Ego -> Character
- You -> Player

What is reality made of and based on?

"If you want to unlock the secret of the universe, you need to think in terms of energy, vibration and frequency". - Nikola Tesla

The world is an ocean of vibration at different frequencies, even matter at the deepest level is vibration at a very slow frequency, so slow that it seems still.

But because we perceive the world through our five senses, we perceive reality through a limited spectrum which manifest as our environment (matter, people, animals, plants, things, sounds, light...), they are all complex structure/framework/organization/bundle of vibration, each of them with they own frequencies. But there is many thing that we don't perceive.

It is comparable to the frequency spectrum found in light and sound, from red to purple, deep tone to high pitched sound, and in each spectrum we can perceive a very limited part of it.

Matter -> Very slow frequency (So it appear still)

Sound -> Rapid frequency (You can only hear a part of it : 20 Hz to 20,000 Hz)

Light -> Very rapid frequency (You can only see a part of it : ~400 nm to ~700 nm)

Sacred geometry

All of creation is based on sacred geometry such as the Flower of Life, the Metatron cube's ... they are dreamed, imagined structure which are the fondation of reality as we know it.

Long story short the Flower of Life (see picture), it is the product of the imagination (**I-magi-nation**) of consciousness, from it emante the Metatron Cube's, and then with the platonic solids which emante from the flower of life and the Metatron Cube's. Each platonics solids represent one of the fives elements; which are the foundation of matter. It is through those sacred geometry that the universe emerged.

There is many more important sacred geometries like you can see :

The vesica Peiscis : It is the first sacred geometric figure to emerge from the creation process
Seed of life : The Seed of Life is a symbol for the seven days of creation. It is found in all major religions and can be seen in many sites e.g. Synagogues, churches, Kabbalah prayer books, and of course, the ancient Osirian temple in Abydos Egypt, the source of all the major religions and mystical studies.
Tree of life: The tree of knowledge, connecting to heaven and the underworld, and the tree of life, connecting all forms of creation, are both forms of the world tree or cosmic tree, and are portrayed in various religions and philosophies as the same tree.
Fibonacci numbers and Golden meaning: There is a special relationship between the Golden Ratio and Fibonacci Numbers (0, 1, 1, 2, 3, 5, 8, 13, 21, ... etc, each number is the sum of the two numbers before it). When we take any two successive (one after the other) Fibonacci Numbers, their ratio is very close to the Golden Ratio: A. B. B / A. . It is the sequence the most found in nature.

I invite you to make your own research about the different sacred geometries and their meanings.

A SMALL GUIDE TO YOURSELF AND TO YOUR DREAMS

The Flower of life

The Metatron Cube's

The platonic solid

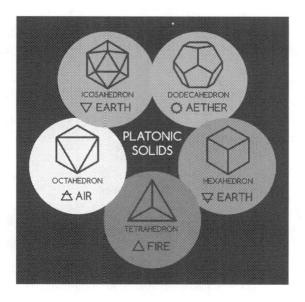

How does reality function?

How can one consciousness have a subjective experience of itself?

This is done through **mirroring**, each subjective aspect work as a mirror for each other and so we all experience our own reflection.

So reality is one big vibratory mirror, reflecting to one s/he vibrational state. What define that state is intentions, thoughts, beliefs system, emotions, actions, focus/attention. Then your vibration state is sent out into the "one-self consciousness network/mirror" and is reflected back at us. Like in a mirror we experience our reflection, only here the mirror is a amazing an complex four dimension reality (4th dimension being time), and the reflection is the experience we have throughout our five senses.

This is known by another name in our society, "the law of attraction", and it state the following, "you attract and experiences people, situation... that are aligned with your frequency/energy/state of being".

The idea is supported from various sources like quantum mechanics, the author Masaru Emoto (who proved that intention had effect of the molecular structure of water, in other word scientific proof of mind over matter once again). Documentaries like "the secret", "what the bleep do we know" and many more.

So inner perception and outer manifestation match to create/ generate the experience that is aligned with your vibrational state/frequency ... may you be conscious or not about it.

–   Obviously if it is done from an unconscious place (identified with the ego and unaware that thoughts shape one's reality) then one experience a reality that is most likely not preferred, a reality of limitation, separation, judgment, label ...
–   On the other hand if it is done consciously (knowing that you are not your thoughts and that they shape your reality) then one can literally experience a dreamlike reality.

Whether you conscious or not if you operate from a place of judgment and label (which usually done from an unconscious state), you perceive reality through the veil/filter of that judgment/label, and therefore your perception distorted version of reality and will probably act unaccordingly, for true reality is what **IS**, without the labeling/judgment of the mind.

So your day to day experience is vibration based, when you experience something you experience a specific frequency that you are/embody.

The world is an ocean of frequencies and you can tape into any of them, all you have to do is be the frequency you want to experience; you want to experience a reality where abundance, love, kindness, excitement, passion, freedom ... then think, believe, feel, behave those things... be the frequency you want to experience and you shall experience them.

Albert Einstein support this fact.

"Be the change you want to see in the world" -Mahatma Gandhi

The process of reflection

There is something I like to call the process of reflection:

Silence -> Imagination -> Choose/Intention ->Belief -> Emotion -> Perception/Manifestation -> Interpretation -> thought -> Action/Behavior

- – *Silence* : All starts with you, for all is within you, you are/contain all of existence, you are silence, consciousness, and you are the creator.

- *Imagine* : From silence arise imagination (I-magi-nation, a nation of magician), and imagination is the catalogue of all that can be experienced.

- *Choose/Intention* : We are born with free-will and the ability to choose. So we can choose the desired experiences.

- *Believe* : Now that you have choosen, you use your beliefs to select the choosen experience. Beliefs act as a selector, it make you tape into certain frequencies.

- *Feel/Emotion*: Your beliefs will give you emotions, and this is what's really going to put your reality into motion (emotion = energy in motion).

- *Perceive* : You then perceive the reality generated/created/selected.

- *Interpretation:* Because you have free will you can interpret what you perceive the way you prefer, and give it meaning.

- *Thought:* Now you might have a thought reaction you what you perceive. Once again it is your job to be conscious of it and let go of those that doesn't serve you and choose/keep those that does. You can also have no thought reaction if you remain highly present.

- *Action/Behavior:* Finally you have action/behavior based on all the above.

So this is the process of reflection, but it requires practice, and that you master your mind at a certain degree.

But I'd like to add the notion of destiny, and that somewhere, somewhat it's all prewritten, the destination is already set, you only get to choose the state of being in which you will reach your destination, in a way.

*"God grant me **the serenity** to accept the things I cannot change, courage to change the things I can, and **wisdom to know the difference**." -Reinhold Niebuhr*

If we restate what was said in the previous chapter "Who are you» **the higher the degree of consciousness the better the perception**", and if we add to that what we just said, it gives us the following.

"The level of consciousness defines the quality of perception, and the beliefs system define the content of what is perceived and experienced." -Cahen Nicolas

DNA

Our emotions have a big influence on our DNA, they can literally reprogram it. There is only two main kind of emotion, love & fear based, and all the spectrum in between, and each emotion have it's own frequency.

Someone living mostly on emotions based on fear, limit s/ he degree of DNA activation because of the low frequency vibration. And so the connection/crossing point with the DNA are rarest. As someone living mostly on emotions based on love will increase the degree of DNA activation because of the high frequency of vibration, which increase the number of connection/crossing point with the DNA.

There is 64 code in our DNA and the average person live with 20, which is not surprising giving the condition in which we grew up. We've been conditioned by the mainstream, which is based on fear, hate, negativity and ignorance.

So now you understand that you have power over your reality, and that you should never react to it (thoughts, peoples, environment) but only reflect. You are the captain of your ship, the author of your story, the music maker of your song...

"Circumstances don't matter, only state of being does, for state of being create circumstances." - Marya Norell

All realities are here and now

Here's an other angle that might help understand how reality works and how to create the one you desire, but before we move forward, we need to clarify a point, **time doesn't exist**.

The present moment is like a room, it's always present, here and now, and what we call time is the movement that happens in that room (people in and out, reading, working, sleeping...)

–   Past: Is a **memory** of something that happened **here and now** but that is over.

- Future: Is a **mental projection** of what could happen **here and now** but haven't yet.

So to conclude, **time is only a mental construct** that isn't real, only **here and now** exist.

Like everything it's not what but how, time can be used as a tool. Past to learn from our mistakes, and the futur to create a vision, launch new ideas, project, goals. But let's not forget, only now exist.

"Yesterday is history, tomorrow is mistery but today is a gift, that's why it's called the present." - Bil Keane

Now that's out of the way, we can move forward and use the following analogy, which is comparing radio stations to realities.

- **You - Physical brain – Reality**
- **You - Radio – Station**

All radio stations are available simultaneously but you can only tune into one at the time, realities work the same way, they are all available simultaneously (here and now) but you can only experience one at the time.

So it just about tuning into the reality that you prefer, and you do that by using your beliefs as your frequency «selector».

From a vibrational standpoint, you CANNOT perceive that which you are not a vibration match to.

You are not the thought "I AM" but the realization "I AM"

There is two fact that if you realize and integrate in your day to day life, they will allow you to be able to make your dreams a reality.

First: **We are not our thoughts... We are the observer.**

Secondly: **Our thoughts are tools of creation, they shape your reality.**

A simple but good and efficient way to start creating a reality to you prefer is to **be positive in words and in thoughts** or to **be silent.**

We don't really need to use the thoughts and words "I am" has much as we think, we can use our thought and word without thinking or speaking "I am's", it actually might be even more efficient in term of communication.

But we live in a world with so many "I am's" that it is understandable to think and speak them, there is actually an interesting book by Joel Osteen called "The power of I AM" who state that what follows "I AM" follows you.

So you can repeat "I am successfull, I am healthy, I am rich, I am beautiful..." activate certain feeling, personnes, objects... as long as it's done consciously and without identification.

But we can address an idear, a need ... without stating that it is you and going strait to the point, for example "Going to buy food" intead of "I am going to buy some food", "Going for a run" instead of "I am going for a run"...

This can sound silly but we have such an "overconsumption" of "I am's" that it's no wonder that so many of us are ego identified, not to mention that creating a conscious reality from that state is not easy task (for we can quicky get drawn into some unconscious, automatic ego habits).

So it is up to you with or without "I am's", **just remember that you are not your thoughts and that they create your reality.**

Act on your passions and excitements

Something else that will help you make your dreams come true is to **act on whatever passionate and excites you the most, for they act like a compass to your path and your trueself,** there is nothing better than being who you are, so always do what passionate and excites you the most in **every given moment.**

Intuition

Something that you can always trust is your intuition or gut feeling, and should learn to trust if it's not already the case. I believe that intuition is the language of the soul, and that we should always listen to it.

Don't want, instead choose, believe, feel, act, receive

You mustn't **want** anything, you must choose, believe, feel, be grateful. Because wanting is a frequencie of **lack**, when you want you say to the univers «**I don't have**» and for all is a mirror, all you will get **is more of not having**.

Instead when you embody what you choose, think it, believe it, feel it, be gratful for it before it manifest, you are in a frequency of abandance, and you will receive more of what you choose.

Also have no expectation, for it act as a filter for the ways in which the Universe can manifest to you what you desire/ choose.

If you expect something to manifest in a certain way, there is little chance for it to actually happen, because by expecting something to happen in a certain way you close all the other doors through which it could happen. So by having no expectation you leave all the doors open and it is easier for the Universe to manifest to you what you choose/desire.

CHAPTER V

SOCIETY

What is a society?

Society is the result of a consensus between people that live together, with this agreement comes a set of guide lines as to create the most integrative, harmonious experience for all. Sadly not all society guide lines are based on integrity but on capitalism...

The current society state

The state of any society is a reflection of the current state of consciousness of it's population; this is true at any scale, town, country, planet...

Since evolution is part of life, our societies evolves too, they are in constant evolution, following some cyclic pattern, from low to high, usually reaching some breaking point from which destruction happens and re-birth of something new arrives, this is comparable at any life form (birth/death, expansion/contraction of the Universe).

*"I mean, it's just. It's the constant, it's the cycle. It's solution, dissolution, just over and over and over. It is **growth**, then **decay**, then transformation." -Walter White*

Today if we should situate ourselves in that evolution cyclic pattern, we would be like **slowly** moving toward adult hood.

Our current society structure/state is obsolete and corrupted, we are living in the past, we follow structure, way of doing, laws that were establish centuries ago that are obsolete and no longer applies, such as the educative system, unsustainable exploitation of resources...

Why and how our society is amiss

We live on a beautiful planet, with beautiful people, the only problem are the wrong intentions, ideas, beliefs, principales, values that have flooded this planet and it's inhabitants.

They are obsolete and belong to an old world, they destroy the planet and do not serve us. Those old ideas beliefs, traditions... have been diffused everywhere including in politics... And so humanity is govern by people that are running inadequate ideas, values, principals...

This originates from dynasty, where "secret" knowledge was passed through the same lineage, keeping the same family in power, knowledge kept away from the people; knowledge that you have just read in the previous chapters.

A SMALL GUIDE TO YOURSELF AND TO YOUR DREAMS

The people in power are not fit for it, hiding true knowledge from the people alone makes you unfit to pocesse it, and we can see that they don't have the peoples best interest at heart, to say the least.

For instance interest of government and corporation are all about money and power at the expense of human lives (Total absence of integrity, values and principals).

This create a sick structure on a society level which create a sick population. What characterizes a sick society structure? **Values out of integrity.**

A very good example is the use of money, in this society money is above all, human lives, animals, environment... and this is reflected in people way of doing, mentalities, today people are ready to do anything for money, disrespect themselves and others...

Another reason why our society is amiss is because the population, **listen** to a corrupted government and **buy** from greedy corporations. Those are important factor as to why our society is broken. The only reason government and corporation have power is because the population give them.

"If no one obeys, no one commands." -Cahen Nicolas

NICOLAS CAHEN

Consequences of corruption and lack of integrity

First of all there is no legitimate elections, for it is the elite community (corporations, lobby's, banks) that "sponsor" political party and define the course of action.

One of the first consequences when the government and corporation are corrupted, and lack of integrity is that they diffusion wrong values, ideas, products...
They broadcast all the ingredient for social conditioning (disinformation, ignorance, unhealthy products...) which create mass identification with the ego at the population level. And today we really have a big population under the influence of this conditioning, without talking about the third world...

As a result society is set up with ideas, notions such as inequality of lives (racism, different social class...), limitation (we all grew up with the notion of scarcity, not enough for everyone), patriotism (justify wars)...

Difference is also shown as a problem, and people are pushed/encouraged to judge themselves, others and to compare themselves with others, when actually everyone's difference is a solution, we are all unique and complementary.

In truth we are all complementary and there is enough of everything for everyone. If we should ever lack anything it would be because of our **aberrant management of resources.** Between what is thrown away by supermarket and restaurant instead of being given to those in need, for no other reason than capitalist values, and between all the food grown for meat production...

Here's the result of an obsolete and corrupted elite community state of mind:

- Fossil fuel (unsustainable)
- School system (obsolete has become more of a ship farms than an educative system)
- Food industry (unsustainable, and where profit is more important that health, human lives, animals life, environment)
- Massive disparity in resources re-partition (Poverty/ Inequality)
- Global warming (result of unsustainable practices)
- Deforestation (no comment)
- Animal slaughter (no comment)
- Human exploitation (no comment)
- Funding of war, and spacial venture instead of resolving the problem of basic needs for each human being.

Transition period

Fortunately we are in a transition period. The old version that was all about exploiting the people and the planet, and all about "ME" (super/victim ego), now we are moving towards a more integrative way of thinking and doing, and it is more about "WE" (integrative ego). Some manifestation of that more integrative period is the implementation of new values, principles, ideas, technology...

For example ecology is becoming a subject that matters, organic food is starting to be a trend, sustainable energy source are starting to bloom, people are starting to care, about their health, the environment...

As for technology, there is a growing number of new innovation, which arrives at an impressive rate, those technology can be used to assist humanity into the next phase of evolution, if used with good intention, like always it's not what but how.

Here are some examples of new technology and ideas:

- Quantum physic
- Quantum computers
- Nano-technology
- Bio-technology
- Artificial intelligence (AI)
- Virtual reality
- Renewable energy
- Blockchain (bring transparency to a lot of fields, including election, allowing to vote without possibility for fraud)
- Alternative source of food production which are sustainable (such a meat cloning, which is a great solution to the over-consumption of meat and the impact it as on the environment, even though this brings ethical questions).

Something that is still much needed is the upgrade of the educative systems, for it is the foundation on which humanity is build in a way. And at the moment we are cultivated and setup in a default mod mindset that correlate with society's needs. Progress as been done by Japan, Finland... but there is still much to do...

We are evolving as a society, and it's exciting, but let's not forget that we all play a part in that evolution, and we all need to contribute at our scale with our unique passions, talents, skills...

And I'd like remind a notion, is that **contrast is required for appreciation.** It is through the dark times that we enjoy the good ones. What would be an eternity of happiness? Eventually nothing, it is only through the existence of struggle, pain and suffering that joy and happiness exist.

What are the solutions?

Earth is a reflection of the collective consciousness of humany, societies work the same way. So to change our society we need to change the principales, values, thinking process and beliefs system of the collective consciousness, this is where the revolution needs to happen, in peoples mind.

So the best way this needs would happen is through upgrading our educative system, it need to be based on integrity, truth... and needs to take into consideration the subjective aspect of each human kind. It need to teach real values and principales that respect living beings and the environment.

It needs to promote diversity, acceptation and to adapt to the uniqueness of each individual, instead of promoting judgment, comparison and trying to make everyone the same, our uniqueness/diversity/difference are complementary and are the source of our strength.

Something else that is needed is **organization**, the reasons why government and corporation are so powerful is because they are organized structured.

So another solution is to create some **official international assembly recognize by the government,** which will allow people to make consensus, through internet for example, social platform...

By doing so we the people would be able to make decisions in a harmonious and efficient way, by voting through an blockchain platform from example for it's unfalsifiability. We could choose representative, based on the integrity of they program, and if they don't respect they it they could be removed through consensus.

We could choose which company we want to see thrive, based on the quality of they products, they environmental footprint, and if they don't meet the requirements we could react with a massive target boycott...

We the people have the power. Just by the number alone, there are more of us, and with great power come great responsibility. All we need is organization on a massive scale.

Because we are living in a capitalism system, it is how we spend our **money**, our **time** and our **energy** that define and shape the society of tomorrow.

So instead of feeding and supporting old structures such as fossil fuels (coal, petrol, gas ..), vehicle with emissions (VE), meat egg and milk industry, fast food, pharmaceutical industry, fear based media ...

One should feed and create new structure based on sustainability and integrity, like purchasing from farmers, new and young entrepreneurs who have integrity and work with ethics. Using renewable energy (solar, wind, ocean, hydro-power, biomass, geothermal, bio-fuels ...), electric cars, eating organic food, watching mind-expanding media content ...

It's through doing those things that the society will change for the better.

Code of ethics

Promote peace	Be positive	Be helpful	Be truthful	Be respectful
Integrity	Do not spread hate	Do not be harmful	Do not be abusive	Be honest

CHAPTER VI

THE ORIGIN OF LIFE

It all started in the timeless, space-less, formless field of existence.

There was a conscious being, who could just be, nothing else, it could not move for is was space-less... And into infinity and eternity it got disinterested, bored and was longing for experiences.

All it could do is dream and imagine, and so it just did that. Through it's dream and imagination it created something called sacred geometries which include the Flower of Life the Metatron Cube's... which allowed that being to create space, time, matter... it is the blueprint of creation.

And so through sacred geometry, the universe and everything that compose it, was created. And this self imagined and dreamed word was created and became the playground of that being.

So that being wasn't bound by it's space-less and formless attributes anymore, it could move through space as pure consciousness. But also as matter, for the ego/avatar (body/

mind-thoughts) was also created, which allowed that being to have a subjective experience of itself, and to move through space, time and interact with it's environment in a very special way.

From here on it started to experience what it could only dream of.

And funny fact from that story, is that you/we/all are that being, and the world around use is our dream. Welcome to your YOU-niverse,

Re-member who you are and have fun.

QUESTIONS THAT CAN HELP YOU GET ON TRACK

If you don't have the life of your dream, and would you like a push in the right direction. I can't achieve it for you but I can help you get there, those questions can help you; Respond with honesty.

- What is your diet? When do you eat? What do you eat for snacks?

- What do you do with your days? What do you spend most of your time on? (Can you describe a typical day).

- Do you exercise, practice any sports?

- Do you get some sunlight every day? Sometimes? Never

- Do you go in nature? Never? Sometimes? Regularly?

- Do you have goals? Short-term, long-term? Are you doing something about it?

- In what environment do you live in? House? Apartment? Clean? Messy? Cozy?

- Do you enjoy the peoples that are in your life? Family? Relationships? Friends? Colleges?

- Do you love your activity and follow your passions, or do a 9-5 to survive?

I am pretty sure than after answering to those questions you might have a few ideas as to what could be wrong. If you feel like it, please send me your answers to cahen.nicolas@gmail.com, I would love to help you.

You can find me on the following social platform

Personal website: https://kn0w-ledge.com

Facebook: https://www.facebook.com/kn0w.ledge.0ne.self/

YouTube: https://www.youtube.com/user/BeerCharger/videos

Twitter: https://twitter.com/CAHENicolas

Truth & Love

One-Self - Nicolas Cahen

ABOUT THE AUTHOR

Nicolas Cahen is a new writer, living between Cape Town, Reunion Island and Paris. His travels gave him the open mind needed to see the world at large. His transcending experiences gives us a unique perspective that is original and refreshing.

He is passionate about philosophy and spirituality which he found himself intensely drawn into around the age of 25.

Printed in the United States
By Bookmasters